nothing

nothing

John Cage and 4'33"

Nicholas Day

ILLUSTRATED BY

Chris Raschka

NEAL PORTER BOOKS
HOLIDAY HOUSE / NEW YORK

For Mila. On whom nothing is lost —N.D.

For Paul and Renate —C.R.

A pianist walks into a barn.

(Don't stop him. He's in the right place.)

The barn is also a concert hall. It's named the Maverick. The pianist is named David Tudor. He's there to play an extraordinary new composition by someone named John Cage.

David Tudor is an extraordinary pianist.

But on this day in 1952, he does not need to be extraordinary at anything.

He just needs to do:

nothing.

David Tudor sits down at the piano.

A bird *chirps.*

A breeze *whistles.*

An audience *stirs.*

And David Tudor does:

noth

ing.

Forty years before David Tudor does nothing, a baby was born in Los Angeles.

The baby had very big ears.

Massive ears.

Even an elephant would look at this baby and say,

Those ears are enormous.

The baby, like the barn, had a name.

The baby's name was John Cage.

The baby's father was an inventor.

And John Cage, when he grew up, invented whole new ways of making music.

He wrote music like no one had ever told him *no*.

But they had.

So he wrote music like he didn't know what *no* meant.

He wrote music in which the only instruments were a dozen radios.

He wrote music for drums and told the musicians to use whatever they wanted. (They used tortoise shells. They used sleigh bells. They used automobile parts.)

He attached screws and bolts and wood and just about everything else to the strings of a piano. And then he played the piano.

The piano sounded like it didn't know what *no* meant.

The piano sounded like a whole lot of *yes*es.

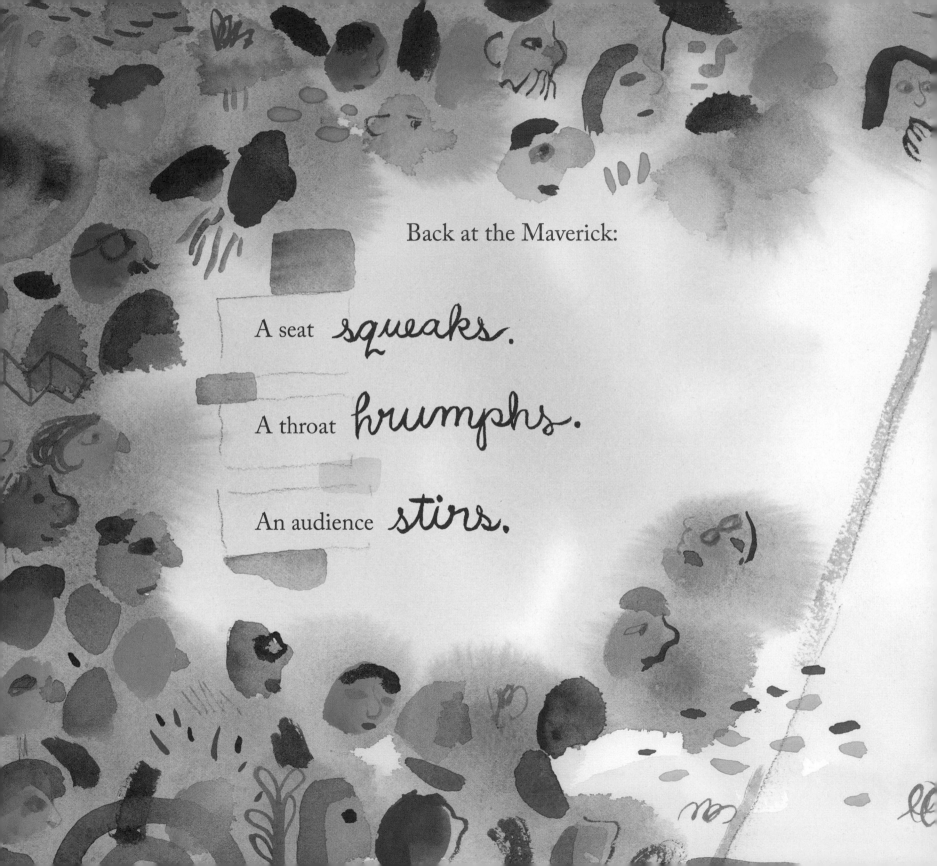

Back at the Maverick:

A seat *squeaks.*

A throat *hrumphs.*

An audience *stirs.*

The audience waits for the part with music.
The audience waits for the part worth listening to.

And David Tudor does:

nothing.

With his massive ears, John Cage heard things that no one else had heard.

He heard what

nothing

sounded like.

He heard that nothing was never nothing.
He heard that there was always something to hear.

A whoosh.

A wheeze.

A whimper.

The sound of yourself, beating underneath it all.

Back at the Maverick:

David Tudor *does something*.

He checks his watch.

A rain *patters.*

A tree *rustles.*

An audience *stirs.*

And then David Tudor does:

nothing.

John Cage wanted to write a piece in which people would hear how much *something* there was in *nothing*.

He wanted people to hear how much *sound* there is in *silence*.

There is always a whole world out there to hear. There is always something to hear inside the silence.

That was what David Tudor was doing at the Maverick: he was letting the audience hear what was inside the silence.

Back at the Maverick:

David Tudor *does*
something else.

He stands up.

The extraordinary
new composition
is over.

And David Tudor
has not played a
single note.

The extraordinary new composition lasts
for four minutes and thirty-three seconds.

John Cage will call it *4' 33"*.

Four minutes and thirty-three seconds
of nothing.

But nothing is never silent.

After the performance, some people in the audience are angry.

We have been *tricked*, they say. They do not use their inside voices. They write upset letters to the newspaper.

But *4' 33"* is not a trick.

And as the years pass, it becomes something unexpected.

It becomes a classic. It is performed before thousands of people at concert halls. It is performed in tiny rooms by rock bands.

And every time, the audience hears something different. They hear whatever there is to hear in that moment.

That is the genius of *4' 33"*.

Every time it is written by the listener. There is always sound in silence. But the composer does not compose those sounds.

The listener *finds* those sounds.

And that listener can be you.

You don't need David Tudor. You don't need a barn.
You don't need a piano.

You only need to make your ears
as big as possible.

And then you just need to do:

noth

About John Cage

"Wherever we are, what we hear is mostly noise. When we ignore it, it disturbs us. When we listen to it, we find it fascinating. The sound of a truck at fifty miles per hour. Static between the stations. Rain."
—John Cage, *Silence*

"Now, Earle, don't you think that John has gone too far this time?"
—John Cage's mother, speaking to the composer Earle Brown after the premiere of *4' 33"*

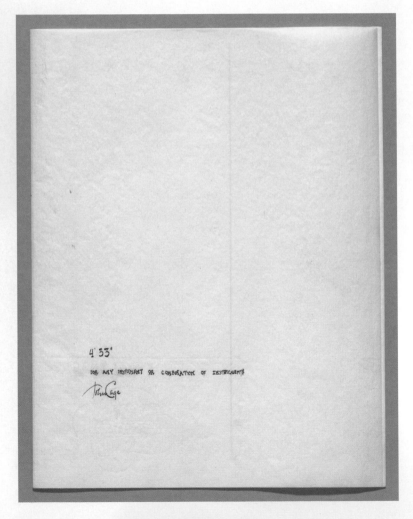

Sheet music for 4' 33", written out by John Cage. Digital Image © The Museum of Modern Art/Licensed by SCALA / Art Resource, NY.

• • •

4' 33" is a blank. Just look at the score, down on the left—there's nothing there.

But listen closely and you can hear the questions it is asking:

What is music?

What is silence?

Can silence be *music*?

Can music be *silence*?

John Cage ranks among the most important American composers of the last century, but he is as famous for his ideas as his music. He is famous for the questions his music asked.

Questions that only seem simple.

Do you have answers to his questions?

Are there even answers to these questions?

For Cage, the questions were always the important part, because the questions were more interesting than the answers. The questions often led to more questions, instead of answers.

Take this simple question:

Who was John Cage?

He was a young radical who became a gentle guru. A rigorous musician who wrote many of his pieces by chance. A figure who was mocked and revered.

A famously noisy composer whose most famous composition was silent.

Who was John Cage?

Are there any simple questions, after all?

• • •

Let us begin with a sturdy fact: John Milton Cage, Jr., was born in Los Angeles, California, on September 5, 1912.

A precocious child, Cage felt out of place his whole California childhood. Even his teachers found him "too interested in reading," he said. He dropped

out of college and left for Europe, where he thought about becoming an artist or an architect. There was a problem: "The people who heard my music had better things to say about it than the people who looked at my paintings had to say about my paintings."

Composer John Cage during his concert held at the opening of the National Arts Foundation, Washington, DC, 1966. Photo by Rowland Scherman/Getty Images

John Cage, 1946. Courtesy of the John Cage Trust.

So he became a composer. It was not a total surprise. Taken to the symphony at the age of five, he stood in the aisle, spellbound, through the entire concert. "I remember loving sound before I ever took a music lesson," he said. "So we make our lives by what we love."

Cage loved sounds that other people hated, or even didn't hear. He composed for percussion orchestras with a bewildering array of instruments that produced a bewildering array of sounds. When recruiting an orchestra became too difficult, Cage invented the prepared piano. It was a seismic invention: it sounded like an orchestra—an orchestra from another world—but it could be played by a single person.

All this brought John Cage to New York, where he had minor fame and next to no money.

But in New York, a pair of men would change Cage's life.

The first was Merce Cunningham, soon to become an iconic modern choreographer. Their relationship, professional and personal, would last the rest of their lives. It would shape Cage's music and Cunningham's dances; it would shape the avant-garde art of the twentieth century.

The second was Daisetz Teitaro Suzuki, a Japanese monk and scholar who is often credited with introducing Zen Buddhism to the United States. Cage attended Suzuki's lectures at Columbia University, and in Zen he found the key he'd been looking for his whole life. The teachings of Zen are often expressed as a series of philosophical puzzles. They are riddles without answers, known as *koans*, and they mirrored the questions that Cage had already been asking. Paradox is central to Zen, and paradox was central to Cage. Only someone comfortable with paradox could write a piece of music with no notes. "I have nothing to say and I am saying it," Cage once wrote. It is a Zen *koan* of his own invention.

4′ 33″ has been compared to *zazen*, or silent meditation. Both are about letting go of expectations and desire and experiencing *this* moment, *this* sound. "What we hear is determined by our own emptiness, our own receptivity," Cage wrote. "We receive to the extent we are empty to do so."

Cage even sought to empty himself out of his own work. It is a seemingly impossible task: a work inevitably reflects the person who made it. But a couple of years before *4′ 33″*, Cage was given a copy of the *I Ching*, the ancient Chinese volume that's both a representation of the universe and a guide to it. The *I Ching* is famously difficult to explain, but for our purposes here, think of it as a way of telling fortunes by flipping a coin. Or more precisely, flipping three coins, six times.

It was this randomness that appealed to Cage. He sometimes used the *I Ching* to make every decision that went into a composition, and a composition requires a lot of decisions. Cage used the *I Ching* to determine the length of *4′ 33″*, for example: rather than an uninterrupted stretch of nothing, the piece is actually a trio of movements, a series of little nothings—33″, then 2′ 40″, then 1′ 20″. (In the inaugural performance, David

Tudor marked the beginning of each movement by *closing* the piano lid.)

With these tools—with these questions—John Cage was ready: he had everything he needed to make *nothing at all*.

He'd thought of a silent piece for years before he dared write it. He was nervous for a lot of good reasons. He was worried people would think it was a joke. He was worried it would ruin his reputation. He was worried he'd never be taken seriously again.

But he felt that *4′ 33″* was too important *not* to write.

What if we listen? What if we *really* listen?

"It seems to me that the activity of modern music has been to open the eyes and the ears of people to things that they were not aware were beautiful," Cage once said. "For instance, in music, particularly to noise."

Shortly thereafter, David Tudor walked into a barn.

He sat down at a piano.

He played nothing.

"It is one of the most intense listening experiences you can have," Tudor said later. "You really listen. You hear everything there is."

Maverick Concert Hall, photographed by Neil Larson.

The people who heard *4′ 33″* started asking their own questions during the performance, when it became clear that Tudor was going to play *nothing*. They talked. They walked. They made, Cage said, "all sorts of interesting sounds."

They became participants in the performance.

There were more questions afterward, when the audience tried to figure out what had just happened. Many people there were musicians who were open to extremely strange new music. They'd just heard a whole concert of it. Before David Tudor sat down at the piano and did *nothing*, he'd played a composition by Cage called *Water Music*. It involves a radio, randomly tuned; a variety of bird whistles; a deck of cards, shuffled; and water poured into a bathtub. (There is also a piano involved.)

Water Music is extremely strange. But it is not *nothing*. And nothing was too much for the audience to bear.

In the angry discussion after the concert, a local artist stood up and said: "Good people of Woodstock, let's drive these people out of town."

It's easy to understand how that artist felt. No one likes to be tricked, and *4′ 33″* can feel like a trick. But it is the opposite. It is extremely earnest. It is wholly sincere. It is the culmination of John Cage's work. It is his diamond, his most important ideas condensed down as far as possible.

He said as much: "The most important piece is my silence piece. Not a day goes by without my making use of that piece in my life and in my work."

He was always listening.

"My favorite music," he liked to say, "is the music I haven't yet heard."

RECORDINGS

Yes, there are recordings of *4' 33"*. There are dozens, in fact. And you can record your own: there is now a *4' 33"* app, released by the John Cage Trust, which allows anyone to record their own versions. On the app and the website, there are hundreds of uploaded recordings from across the globe. You can hear water in Denali National Park in Alaska. Voices outside Mumbai. Night in Rwanda. A party in Iceland. A train in Taiwan.

And then you can share your own moment in the world. Your own patch of sound. Your own 4 minutes and 33 seconds.

BIBLIOGRAPHY

Cage, John. *Silence: Lectures and Writings*. Middletown, CT: Wesleyan University Press, 2011.

Gann, Kyle. *No Such Thing as Silence: John Cage's 4' 33"*. New Haven, CT: Yale University Press, 2011.

Kostelanetz, Richard. *Conversing with Cage*. New York: Routledge, 2003.

Larson, Kay. *Where the Heart Beats: John Cage, Zen Buddhism, and the Inner Life of Artists*. New York: Penguin, 2012.

Revill, David. *The Roaring Silence: John Cage, A Life*. London: Bloomsbury, 1992.

John Cage: Journeys in Sound. Directed by Allan Miller and Paul Smaczny. Accentus Music, 2012.

Neal Porter Books

Text copyright © 2024 by Nicholas Day
Illustrations copyright © 2024 by Chris Raschka
All Rights Reserved
HOLIDAY HOUSE is registered in the U.S. Patent and Trademark Office.
Printed and bound in December 2023 at Toppan Leefung, DongGuan City, China.
The artwork for this book was created with watercolor, pencil, and ink on paper.
Book design by Jennifer Browne
www.holidayhouse.com
First Edition
1 3 5 7 9 10 8 6 4 2

Library of Congress Cataloging-in-Publication Data

Names: Day, Nick (Nicholas) author. | Raschka, Christopher, illustrator.
Title: Nothing : John Cage and *4' 33"* / Nicholas Day, Chris Raschka.
Description: First edition. | New York : Neal Porter Books / Holiday House, 2024. | Audience: Ages 4–8 | Audience: Grades K–1 | Summary: "The story of the composer John Cage's famous composition of four minutes and 33 seconds of empty sheet music, and its first performance by the pianist David Tudor"— Provided by publisher.
Identifiers: LCCN 2023011269 (print) | LCCN 2023011270 (ebook) | ISBN 9780823454099 (hardcover) | ISBN 9780823457601 (ebook)
Subjects: LCSH: Cage, John. *4' 33"*, no. 1—Juvenile literature. | Silence—Juvenile literature.
Classification: LCC ML3930.C18 D29 2024 (print) | LCC ML3930.C18 (ebook) DDC 780.92 [B]—dc23/eng/20221011
LC record available at https://lccn.loc.gov/2023011269
LC ebook record available at https://lccn.loc.gov/2023011270

ISBN 978-0-8234-5409-9 (hardcover)